My Daddy is DE

By Brandy Marik

To Alyssa and her favorite Hero.

I'm as lucky as I can be,
The best daddy in the world
belongs to
ME.

But when he goes on a trip,

I think sometimes I might just flip!

My mommy says that he's
D-E-P-L-O-Y-E-D.
That word makes me very
A-N-N-O-Y-E-D!

I say, "I want my daddy back now!"
My mommy smiles and asks, "but how?"

Maybe we could go and get him

ON A PLANE!

OR
maybe we could go and get him

ON A TRAIN!

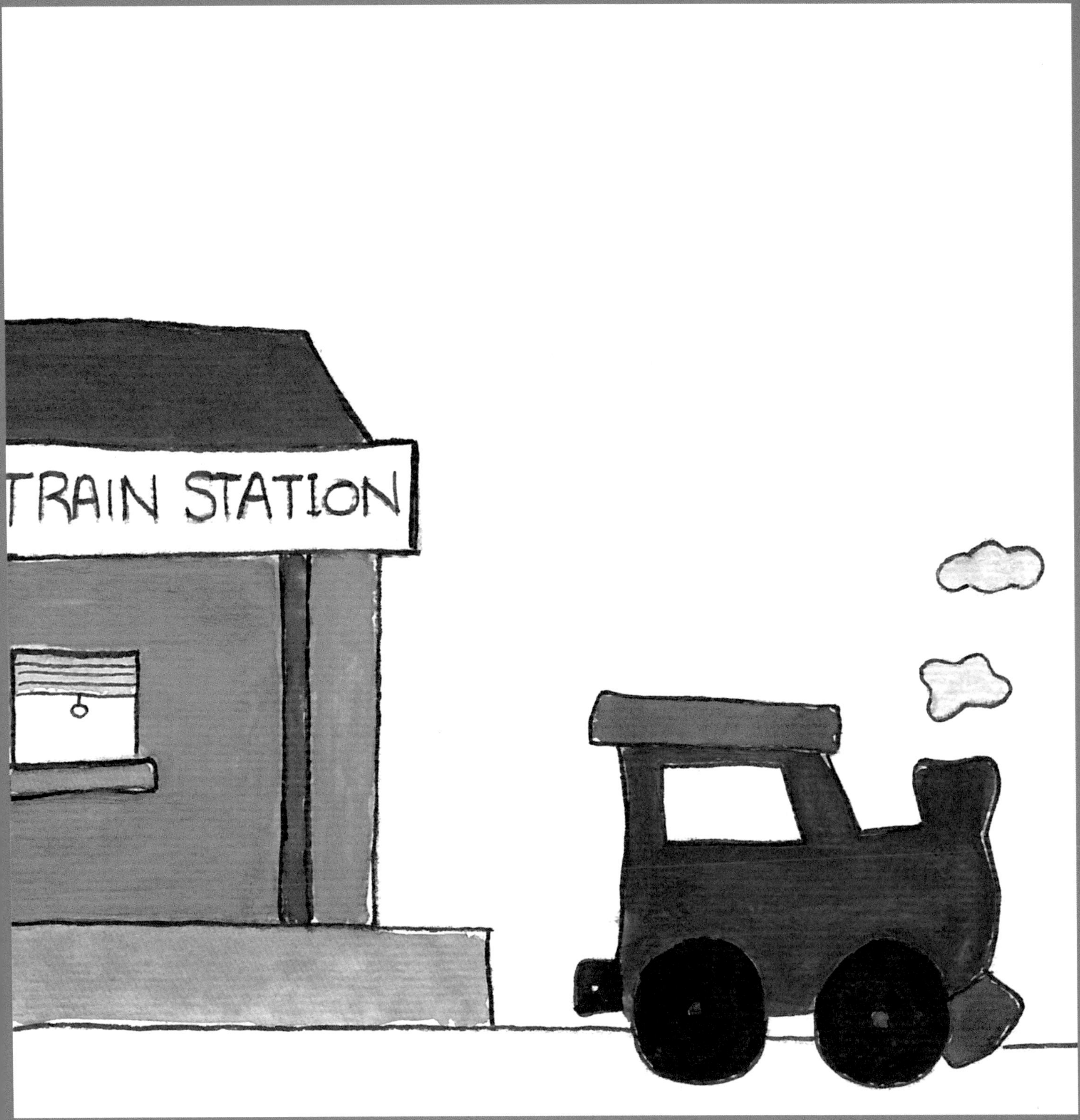
TRAIN STATION

Maybe we could go and get him

ON A SHIP!

"Oh my", says mommy, "that would be

A VERY LONG TRIP!"

I wonder how surprised

he would be

to SEE,

I am there

to bring him home

with ME!

Deployments
take TOO long.

My mommy says
we have to be strong.

We'll send lots of pictures
so he can see me smile,
We will even get to talk to him
once in a while.

Before we know it, time will fly by,
And soon we will be saying
HELLO
instead of
GOODBYE.

Oh how I'm dreaming of that day,
When my daddy is safe at home to stay!
I will hug him as tight as I possibly can.
I will say,
"I LOVE YOU DADDY.
YOU ARE MY HERO
AND I AM YOUR BIGGEST FAN!"

Made in the USA
Middletown, DE
13 July 2017